Remnants: A Journey Through Grief, Love And Becoming

Aarti Upadhyay

BookLeaf Publishing

India | USA | UK

Copyright © Aarti Upadhyay
All Rights Reserved.

This book has been self-published with all reasonable efforts taken to make the material error-free by the author. No part of this book shall be used, reproduced in any manner whatsoever without written permission from the author, except in the case of brief quotations embodied in critical articles and reviews.

The Author of this book is solely responsible and liable for its content including but not limited to the views, representations, descriptions, statements, information, opinions, and references ["Content"]. The Content of this book shall not constitute or be construed or deemed to reflect the opinion or expression of the Publisher or Editor. Neither the Publisher nor Editor endorse or approve the Content of this book or guarantee the reliability, accuracy, or completeness of the Content published herein and do not make any representations or warranties of any kind, express or implied, including but not limited to the implied warranties of merchantability, fitness for a particular purpose.

The Publisher and Editor shall not be liable whatsoever...

Made with ❤ on the BookLeaf Publishing Platform
www.bookleafpub.in
www.bookleafpub.com

Dedication

To Maa, Papa, my brother, and my bhabhi—thank you for your love, strength, and unwavering belief in me. And to Grief—for the lessons learned. This book is yours.

Preface

Grief is a universal language, yet it speaks differently to each one of us. It is a journey, a process which we must undertake alone as no two people have the same lived experience.

This collection was born from the fragments of my own experiences with loss, love, of loss of love, followed by a messy, beautiful process of healing. It is shaped by the conversations I have had with my friends, my family and my psychiatrist while navigating grief. It is a tribute to the people I've lost, the broken dreams I've mourned, and the parts of myself I've had to rebuild, with a little help from my 'safe spaces'. These poems are not just about grief; they are about the resilience that emerges from it, the small acts of kindness that keep us going, and the quiet strength we find when we choose to keep living.

If you are navigating grief, know that your pain is valid, your healing is your own, and your story is still being written. May these words offer you solace, a moment of connection, and a gentle reminder that even in the midst of sorrow, there is light. You are not broken beyond repair—you are becoming.

With love, hope and strength,
Aarti Upadhyay

Acknowledgements

To my psychiatrist, Dr. Sarthak Dave—my deepest gratitude for guiding me through the shadows of grief with such compassion, patience, and insight.

To my dear friends, Nirwa Mehta and John Benny—your unwavering presence throughout this journey, both in life and in writing, has meant more than words can express. Your encouragement and belief in me sustained me through the hardest moments. You read my rawest thoughts, stood by me without hesitation, and reminded me that I wasn't alone.

And to Animish Raje, my very first reader—thank you for your keen eye and thoughtful feedback.

This book would not exist without each of you. Thank you for walking this path with me.

1. Crossroads of Silence

The first day after you left,
my world shattered, clean and swift.
A hollow echo where your laughter rang,
an empty space where our two souls sang.

I stood at a crossroads, lost and bare,
a mapless traveler in despair.
Each path a blur, a hazy line,
no compass pointing, no star to shine.

Have you ever felt so utterly alone,
stripped of connection, heart turned to stone?
The weight of loneliness, a crushing blow,
the bitter taste of having nowhere to go.

Being left behind, a cruel, sharp sting,
the sudden knowledge that no bells will ring
to call you back, no hand to hold,
just empty silence, stark and cold.

The air grew heavy, thick with unshed tears,
a suffocating blanket of my fears.
I couldn't breathe, each breath a fight,
and prayed for darkness, prayed for night.

For in the shadows, maybe then,
this aching emptiness would end.
Or maybe, just maybe, I could find,
a flicker of strength left behind.

2. A Cry for Help

My heart claws at my ribs,
a caged thing thrashing,
begging for quiet—
for anything but this.

Every hour, a chase,
running from shadows,
filling the silence with noise,
with motion, with nothing.

My hands stay busy,
but my mind—
it slips through the cracks,
spilling into the dark.

I bury memories in the grind,
shovel dirt over ghosts,
but they rise, again and again,
to whisper your name.

You are gone.
Not missing, not lost—
just gone.
A phantom limb I still try to move.

So I keep running,
keep drowning in distractions,
hoping exhaustion will swallow the ache,
hoping sleep will be kind.

But the weight stays.
The scream stays.
And no one hears it but me.

3. When Grief Became My Body

Sleep was the first to leave,
slipping away like a tide at dusk,
no lullaby, no quiet peace,
just endless nights wrapped in rust.

Hunger turned to a foreign land,
once familiar, now unknown,
each bite a distant memory,
as emptiness became my own.

My eyes, rivers run dry,
burning from the salt of sorrow,
blinking against the weight of loss,
dreading the coming of tomorrow.

My bones—hollow, heavy, still,
as if they carried echoes deep,
a silence loud, a whisper sharp,
a weariness I could not keep.

My heart, a trembling wreck,
crushed beneath an unseen weight,
aching in a way so vast,

no measure could translate.

My mind, a fog-bound shore,
where thoughts dissolved, adrift,
the world once bright and clear,
now veiled in shadow's shift.

For days, for nights, for weeks it stayed,
medicine whispered but did not mend,
until exhaustion met resolve,
and I sought a guiding hand to lend.

Grief had made a home in me,
filled my bones, my breath, my skin,
but seeking help, I turned the key,
to let the light back in.

4. Echoes of Hope

In the shadow of your love, I once stood,
Beneath the weight of your hot, then cold mood.
You were the sun, and I, the parched earth,
Craving your warmth, fearing your dearth.

I leapt for the hope, like a flame to the moth,
Believing each smile was not a mere broth.
But a promise, a sign, that love would prevail,
A cycle of joy, through a storm's gale.

I waited, oh how I waited, for that moment so rare,
When your eyes would soften, and you'd show you care.
Each flicker of kindness, I cherished, I saved,
Believing this time, your love would be braved.

Hopeless hoping against all the signs,
Ignoring the clocks, the endless times.
I clung to the moments, so far, so few,
Each one a treasure, each one anew.

But the wait was a desert, vast and so long,
The pain of wanting, sharp and strong.
I mistook your breadcrumbs for a feast,
Chasing a mirage, seeking the least.

Now I see, through tears and through pain,
That love shouldn't hurt, shouldn't strain.
I'm learning to heal, to let go, to mend,
From the trauma bond, to find my own end.

The joy was fleeting, the pain was real,
But from this darkness, I'll surely heal.
For I am more than the sum of your cold,
I am warmth, I am love, I am whole.

5. Encountering Empathy

In the quiet room of healing minds,
A conversation, tender, unwinds.
I speak, my voice both firm and light,
Of paths I've walked, of my days and nights.

"I am Aarti," I softly state,
Leading with vision, clearing the haze,
Turning ideas into paths well-lit,
Helping my team to create, and commit.

I love to write, to weave words into art,
But life's heavy with a decade's dark part.
A toxic love, now left behind,
Its shadows linger, hard to unbind.

"I want to move on," I confesses with pain,
"To feel normal, to love myself again."
To forgive the years, I spent in chains,
A wish to heal, to feel no more strains.

How will you do that?" the doctor asks,
I sit in silence, the question vast.
Tears rise, heavy with the past,
A love once clung to, now held as ash.

The doctor speaks, with wisdom and care,
"To heal, you must sit with despair."
"For a week, don't battle your heart's cry,
Embrace your emotions, let them not lie."

"Just sit with your pain," he gently guides,
"Listen to what it tries to confide."
A week to pass, with emotions in tow,
A journey through pain, to eventually grow.

Thus, in this space where healing begins,
I find hope, and perhaps, new wins.

6. Grief's Grip

"How did you feel," doctor asked, his voice so calm,
"When the news broke, that unexpected balm?"
I told him then, the clock had struck eleven,
Fifteen past, a message sent from heaven,
Or hell, perhaps, I couldn't quite decide,
Just that the world within me, shifted wide.

No sleep that night, the thoughts a swirling storm,
I called my brother, seeking some kind of warm,
Reassurance, comfort, but the dam gave way,
A meltdown's torrent, washing night away.
Then Facetime's glow, a friend's familiar face,
Another breakdown, in that lonely space.

My mother's voice, a lifeline in the dark,
But even love could not relight the spark.
Four in the morning, still I lay awake,
My weary soul, about to break.
Five AM arrived, I tried to close my eyes,
But sleep eluded me, beneath the dawning skies.

The next day dragged, exhaustion took its hold,
I pushed myself at work, a story to be told,
Of tiredness conquered, sleep that would descend,

But even then, the night brought no amend.

"Shall I prescribe," he asked, with gentle tone,
"Some sleeping pills, to help you feel less prone
To this insomnia, this relentless plight?"
"Do I need them?" I questioned, in the fading light.

He paused, considering, "There's collateral cost,
A price to pay, for something gained and lost.
You're grieving now, your heart is raw and bare,
Your full capacity, you cannot fully share.
In work, in life, it's natural to slow,
This pain you feel, in time, it will go.
Give it some time," he said, with knowing grace,
"The wounds will heal, at their own steady pace."

7. The Pace of Healing

Two weeks pass, and here we sit,
The clock ticks soft, the room stays lit.
"How are you now?" he gently pries,
"Surviving," I say, no need for lies.

A knowing smile, a quiet pause,
"That's the most honest answer, because—
Most people lie when I ask them this,
They dress their pain in counterfeit bliss."

I don't wait, I spill my thought,
"I don't want to feel this, not what it brought."
The silence lingers, but I press on,
"How much time until this is gone?"

Again, he smiles—calm, composed,
"I never answer that, you know."
"Then tell me, how long for a fracture to mend?"
"Depends on the injury," I say, like a friend.

"No," he corrects, his voice like rain,
"It takes as much time as it needs.
You cannot rush what aches and grieves,
You must sit with it, let it breathe."

A pause, a shift, a measured stare,
"Tell me, are you certain, aware—
That you don't want to turn around?
What if this is just a pause, not the final sound?"

The past knocks softly, but I don't move,
"It already ended, and I won't undo."
No hesitation, no blurred lines,
No longing left between the signs.

He nods, the faintest grin in place,
"Then let's move forward, at your pace.
With patience, emotions will rise and fall,
You'll feel too much; you'll feel it all.
But if you keep going, let time extend...
One day, this will surely end."

8. Echoes of Absence

In the quiet morning light, there's a hollow space beside me,
Where once warmth lay, now only emptiness resides.
I wake with tears, a silent river on my cheeks,
Realizing anew the void where love once spoke.

The day begins, but the sun feels cold,
Without your laughter, your voice, the stories you told.
Each sip of chai, a bitter taste of absence,
The steam rising like memories we'll no longer share.

Meals are solitary now, the table too wide,
For one, where once we sat side by side.
Every bite reminds me of your favorite dish,
The joy of cooking for two, now a dish for one.

Through the day, I navigate a world halved,
The mundane moments, once shared, now feel like theft.
Your absence is in every breath, every step,
A constant, painful reminder of the love that left.

The evening comes, and with it, the stark reality,
That the anchor of my days, my guide,
Is gone, leaving me to drift in this vast sea,

Of memories, of love, of the life we built inside.

This emptiness, this silent sorrow, this profound loss,
Teaches me the depth of love, the cost of its absence.
Each day, a journey through the empty rooms of my
heart,
Learning to live with what we were, what we are no
more.

9. The Void

Have you ever gaped at the void?
Not just looked, but really seen it—
Felt its weight, its silence, its stretch beyond knowing.

It is vast, too vast,
Not just emptiness but an absence,
A space shaped like someone who is no longer there.

I try to fill it.
With memories—flashes of laughter, echoes of a voice,
Moments that once felt endless but now feel like
borrowed time.

But how long can the mind replay them?
How long can I hold onto something that no longer
grows?

I wait.
For the void to shift, to shrink, to whisper back.
But maybe it does not shrink—maybe it just settles,
Filling itself with time, with breath, with something I
don't understand yet.

10. December 2020

COVID took many things from me.
Career stability, a sense of control,
Threw me into a world I didn't know,
A job that felt unfamiliar, a life that felt uncertain.

But I never thought it would take you.

I was recovering, alone in a room,
Counting days, waiting for the fever to break.
And then came the news—
Not a phone call, not a moment to prepare,
Just words that didn't make sense.

You were gone.
Just like that.

December 2020 was cold,
Colder than any winter I had known.
Not just in the air, but in my bones,
In the empty space where your presence should have
been.

Five years now.
I am still here, still waiting—

For what, I don't know.
For it to make sense? For the weight to lift?
For time to do what everyone says it will?

But grief doesn't listen to time.
It just stays,
Like winter that never really leaves.

11. The Night Walk

I walk alone.
Rain pours, cold and endless,
Drenching my skin, seeping into my bones.
No place to go, no shelter, just the sound of water
And the quiet ache of loss.

Tears mix with the rain.
She is gone—my neighbour, my childhood's familiar
voice.
Grief presses against my chest, but I keep walking.
The road is long, the night endless.

And then, a temple.
Golden light spills through the dark,
And there, waiting, is Dadi.
Gone for 25 years, yet standing before me,
As real as the storm around us.

I bow.
To the idol, to her, to something I cannot name.
The rain still falls, but for a moment,
There is warmth.

And then I wake—

Tears on my face, fear in my heart.
Who will I lose next?

21

12. Chai and Samosa – A Promise

Shilpi never let anyone leave empty-handed.
Her door, always open, her warmth, always steady.
And chai and samosa—her little ritual of love.
Crisp, golden, steaming cups of comfort,
Laughter rising like the aroma of ginger and cardamom.

The last time I saw her,
She smiled, "Come, let's have chai and samosa."
But I was late—life pulling me away.
"Next time," I had said.
Not knowing that time had already closed its door.

Now, I wait.
For another place, another time, another life.
A table set with chai, samosas, and her smile.
It is a promise.

13. Where Do I Put This Love?

I carry it all—
The love, the joy, the stories never told,
The moments that could have been,
The life I built in my mind with you.

But where do I put it now?
This love that has no home,
These words that have no ear,
These hands that reach for nothing?

Grief lingers like an unfinished song,
A melody trapped in silence.
What do I do with it?
Where do I take the love that has nowhere to go?

I hold it.
I let it ache.
I let it be mine.

14. A Follow Up Conversation

In the quiet room where shadows softly weep,
I sat with my doctor, my secrets to keep.
I spoke of the heartache, the pain, the despair,
Of a love that was lost, of a soul laid bare.

I called him narcissistic, self-centered, unkind,
A man who was deaf to the cries of my mind.
But my doctor leaned forward, his voice calm and clear,
"Do labels heal wounds, or keep the pain near?"

He said, "Your healing is not in his name,
Nor in the shadows of his selfish game.
To mend your heart, you must turn within,
Where your emotions reside, where your truth begins."

"Feel what you feel, let no tear be denied,
Each ache, each anger, each grief you've cried.
Acknowledge their presence, let them have their say,
For they are the guides on your healing way."

"He did what he could, though it caused you pain,
Now it's your turn to break free from the chain.
The focus is you, not him, not his role,

But the reclaiming of your fragmented soul."

"Observe each feeling, let it speak its part,
For every emotion is a piece of your heart.
They're not here to harm you, but to help you see,
The path to your healing, the path to be free."

I left with a whisper, a spark in my chest,
A newfound resolve to face this quest.
No longer his prisoner, no longer his muse,
I'll heal for myself, with the strength I choose.

For labels may linger, but they won't define,
The light that I'm seeking, the peace I'll find.
And so I'll move forward, one feeling at a time,
To a future unburdened, a life that's mine.

15. My Sadness Wears Black

My sadness wears black—
a shade so deep, it swallows the light.
She moves like a shadow,
silent, steady, misunderstood.

People call her trouble,
say she lingers too long,
say she is cruel, ruthless—
but they don't know her like I do.

She's never lied to me,
never sugar-coated the weight in my chest.
When loss knocks, when tension coils,
she's the one who stays.

She doesn't cheer or pretend,
doesn't ask me to fake a smile.
She just sits beside me,
letting me be.

And yet, I push her away,
hide her under distractions,
treat her like an unwelcome guest—
while joy, excitement, love get all my warmth.

It's unfair, really.
She only ever wanted to teach me,
to show me what matters,
to remind me I feel because I live.

So maybe tonight,
I'll let her stay a little longer,
sip the silence with her,
and listen.

16. When Joy Knocked

Grief sat heavy, a quiet ghost,
wrapped around my ribs, weighing my steps.
I carried her with me, everywhere—
to work, to home, to silence.

Then chai. A break. A breath.
Huddled with my team, steam rising,
voices swirling like warm monsoon winds.
A joke—silly, light, unexpected.

Laughter cracked the air,
sudden, wild, free.
Before I knew it, I laughed too—
a sound I hadn't heard in days.

And then, a pang.
Guilt curled its fingers around my throat.
Was it written somewhere
that joy and grief cannot sit at the same table?

Had I betrayed my sorrow?
Turned my back on what was lost?
Or was this just life, slipping through,
reminding me I am still here?

Joy did not demand to stay.
She only knocked,
brushed against my heart,
and left the door open.

And maybe, just maybe,
I will let her in again.

17. Love, Despite It All

If love is scarce,
shouldn't that be reason enough
to pour it freely,
to give it like air,
without measure, without weight?

And yet, we falter.
We hold it close, ration it,
offer it only when it feels safe,
when it fits our shape,
when it loves us back in the way we crave.

We meet people,
not where they stand,
but where we wish they were.
We dress them in our expectations,
then grieve when they don't fit.

We ask for more
before learning their burdens,
forgetting that love is not a currency
but a gift, a shelter, a warmth
given with no debt to collect.

Perhaps love is not missing—
only misplaced,
lost in the spaces
where acceptance should be,
buried beneath what we demand
instead of what we offer.

So let us love, despite it all.
Despite the distance, the flaws, the fears.
Let us love, not for what we receive,
but for what we become
when we do.

18. The Mind Remembers, Then Forgets

"You know," the doctor said,
leaning back in his chair,
"Our minds are wired
to chase the freshest wound."

Grief feels endless—
a storm that will not break,
but then, something new arrives,
a task, a worry, a moment demanding more.

And just like that,
what once felt unbearable
slips quietly to the back row,
not gone, but waiting,
a shadow among many.

It isn't healing, not really.
Not a grand epiphany,
not the weight lifting,
not an act of will.
Just the mind, shifting,
choosing survival without asking permission.

I wanted to argue,
to insist that my grief was different,
that it could not be moved,
that it was too much, too heavy, too real.

But somewhere between breaths,
between showing up,
between holding on,
I realized—

I had already let go
without meaning to.

19. A Cosmic Truth

The path we walked, a ribbon bright,
Through sunlit days and shadowed night,
A tapestry of laughter shared,
And burdens that we bravely bared.

We learned the lessons, deep and true,
The universe its wisdom drew,
From every glance, each spoken word,
A silent symphony we heard.

Then, subtly, the path diverged,
A gentle hand, the pages urged,
To close the chapter, soft and low,
A quiet "goodbye," a letting go.

No bitter words, no harsh farewell,
Just fading echoes, like a bell,
That rings and fades into the air,
Leaving a memory, sweet and rare.

"The Last Meeting," whispers low,
A cosmic truth, we start to know,
That every soul we intertwine,
Has purpose, in the grand design.

And though we yearn for what has been,
The universe, serene and keen,
Has woven fates, with careful hand,
And led us to a different land.

So let the memories softly gleam,
A cherished fragment of a dream,
For in that parting, we are free,
To grow and blossom, wild and glee.

No looking back, no vain regret,
The lessons learned, we can't forget,
And though our paths may never meet,
Our journey's end, bittersweet.

20. The Secret Language of Dark Emotions

We shun the shadows, fear the night,
Emotions dark, that dim the light.
We label them as foes unkind,
And seek a happiness defined,
By constant joy, a sunlit sky,
Ignoring whispers passing by.

But anger's flame, a burning brand,
A call to action, close at hand.
It signals wrongs that must be righted,
A voice suppressed, now reunited.

Disappointment, a somber hue,
A gentle nudge, to see things through.
It whispers softly, "Don't give in,"
Persistence is the path to win.

Anxiety, a fluttering wing,
A nervous tremor, what will spring?
It's not a monster, fierce and grim,
But preparation's gentle hymn.

Guilt, a weight upon the soul,

A debt unpaid, a missing goal.
It's not to crush, or cause despair,
But mend the rift, and show we care.

And pain, the sharpest, keenest sting,
A revelation it can bring.
Where hurts the most, a truth resides,
The compass of our heart, it guides.
It shows us values, deep and true,
What matters most, in all we do.

So let us not these feelings scorn,
But see the lessons they adorn.
For in the darkness, light can bloom,
And wisdom rise from every gloom.
Embrace the shadows, understand,
The messages held in their hand.
They're not our enemies, but friends,
Who help us grow, until the end.

21. The First Day of Recovery

The night was kind, it let me rest,
A gentle sleep—no weary test.
The weight I carried, heavy, deep,
Was lighter now—I dared to breathe.

January's breeze ran through my hair,
Crisp and soft, a whispered care.
The world, once distant, dull, and gray,
Began to bloom in light that day.

Chai was warm, the spices true,
Food had flavor, rich and new.
Words returned—I held my pen,
Felt like writing once again.

Arms embraced, love held me tight,
Familiar warmth, a soul set right.
And for the first time in so long,
I wished to hear a tale, a song.

Not whole, not healed, but on my way,
A glimpse of normal, bright and brave.

Recovery knocked—a soft hello,
And I smiled, just letting go.

22. The Last Good Bye

He says, "You're leaving..."
His voice, a fragile thread,
She replies, soft, deceiving,
"You only said you had work in the afternoon instead."

Her hand finds his, a quiet plea,
A bridge between the unspoken,
She sits, her heart a silent sea,
His eyes, so wide, so broken.

She watches, tracing thoughts he hides,
The weight of words unsaid,
A storm beneath his gaze resides,
But neither turns their head.

Two minutes pass, or maybe three,
Time stretches, thin and frail,
She whispers, "I'll book the cab, you see,"
Her voice begins to trail.

A peck upon his cheek she leaves,
A fleeting, tender spark,
The cab arrives, and though it grieves,
She steps into the dark.

He hugs her tight, a final breath,
"Bye," he murmurs low,
She knows this kiss is the goodbye kiss,
The end of all they know.

A tear escapes, a silent cry,
As she walks away, unseen,
Not in this life, nor when they die,
Will their paths cross again.

The cab rolls on, the night descends,
Her heart, a shattered pane,
For love begins, but love also ends,
And nothing stays the same.

23. Malleable, Yet Mighty

"Water's malleable," I sighed,
"It takes the shape of what's inside.
A cup, a cloud, a flowing stream,
It bends and shifts, a fluid dream.
Heated, it vanishes in air,
Tinted by hues it changes near.
I'm a water sign, you see,
This shapeshifting... isn't me."

He smiled, "But water's more than this,
It's energy, pure, boundless bliss.
The most essential, strong, and true,
And here's the secret, known to few:
No matter how it's forced to change,
It always finds its original range.

You boil it, steam ascends on high,
But rain returns, from cloudy sky.
That's water's strength, its core so deep,
Life's very essence, secrets to keep.
No life exists where water's not,
A vital force, misunderstood, I thought.

So be like water, friend of mine,

Adaptable, resilient, and divine.
Let circumstances shift and sway,
Your true self will light the way.
Return to center, strong and free,
Like water, you're meant to be."

24. The Gift Denied

A battlefield within my skull resides,
Where past replays, and future plans collide.
My mind, a foe, it wages constant war,
Ignoring now, the precious gift I pour.

The ghost of yesterday, it haunts my thought,
Each misstep etched, a lesson dearly bought.
Regrets they linger, whispers in the breeze,
Stealing the joy, and robbing inner peace.

Then future beckons, a mirage so bright,
A promised land, bathed in a hopeful light.
I build my castles, in the clouds so high,
Forgetting present, as the moments fly.

This tug-of-war, this endless, restless chase,
Leaves me adrift, in this forgotten space.
The present moment, a fleeting butterfly,
I try to grasp it, but it flutters by.

Why does this hope, of what is yet to be,
Eclipse the now, and blind me, can't I see?
This constant yearning, for a future's gleam,
Extinguishes the fire, of life's vibrant dream.

When will I find, this clarity I crave?
This stillness deep, where troubled waters wave
Will calm at last, and peace begin to bloom,
And banish shadows, from this mental tomb?

When will I learn, to silence inner strife,
And truly cherish, this ephemeral life?
To let go gently, of what has been,
And what might be, and simply just be within?

To breathe this air, to feel this sun's warm kiss,
To find contentment, in this very bliss.
To be present, honest, and truly real,
And let the present, my wounded spirit heal.

25. The Girl Who Feared Joy

She longed for joy, a fleeting light,
A spark to pierce her endless night.
Yet when it came, so soft, so near,
Her heart would tremble, gripped by fear.

For happiness, a fragile thread,
Would whisper tales of dread instead.
"What if it leaves? What if it fades?
What if I'm trapped in darker shades?"

She told herself, "You don't belong,
In fields of laughter, in songs of song.
For every smile, a tear must fall,
To balance joy, to pay it all."

And so she wept, though unaware,
Her mind a labyrinth, a snare.
She sought the shadows, clung to pain,
For joy, she thought, was not her gain.

A victim of patterns, of cycles spun,
By hands unseen, by battles won.
Her mind, a jailer, cruel and sly,
Would steal the sun from her sky.

Yet in her depths, a quiet plea,
A hope that one day she'd be free.
To hold the light, to let it stay,
To greet the dawn, not fear the day.

For joy is not a debt to pay,
Nor must it always slip away.
It's hers to claim, to hold, to keep,
A treasure vast, an ocean deep.

Oh, gentle soul, so bruised, so kind,
Release the chains that bind your mind.
For you deserve the light you seek,
The joy you fear, the peace you need.

And though the path may twist and bend,
Your heart, in time, will learn to mend.
For joy is yours, as vast as skies,
A gift no fear should ever disguise.

26. My Unpaid Therapist

You're the one who hears my silence,
A listening ear when storms arise,
The steady hand that guides me through,
A lighthouse in my darkest skies.

You feed my joy with gentle words,
A smile that melts my heaviest fears,
When crisis calls, you stand so close,
A fortress built through all these years.

I jump headfirst into my abyss,
Yet you're the rope that pulls me free,
With compassion deep, you light my way,
A mirror of the best in me.

You take my contradictions, raw,
The mess I am, the fights within,
And weave them into something whole,
A peace that lets me breathe again.

Though miles may stretch between our worlds,
You're just a call, a voice away,
A bridge that spans the distance wide,
A constant in my disarray.

You'd move the earth to see me smile,
My battles yours, my wins your own,
My enemies you claim as yours,
And celebrate all my wins.

Oh, friend, my unpaid therapist,
My anchor, light, and truest guide,
In you, I've found a love so rare,
A heart that walks forever by my side.

27. The Power of Small Eyes

They called her names, they mocked her face,
Laughed at her eyes, so small, so misplaced.
"Chinky, Nepali, Bhutani too,
Manipurian—oh, the names just grew."

Yet, she stood tall, a smirk so wide,
Never once let the hurt reside.
"You fools," she'd say, "you fail to see,
The power these small eyes hold in me."

"They're windows vast, they stretch so far,
Past every taunt, beyond each scar.
Japan, China, Korea's grace,
Thailand, Nepal—I hold their space."

She didn't invent it, but she believed,
A boy once whispered, and she received—
"Your eyes aren't small, they're vast, they're grand,
They hold whole nations in their span."

So laugh if you must, but know this right,
Her world is bigger, her soul burns bright.
For in those eyes, deep and true,
Lies a vision far beyond their view.

28. A Cup of Indigo

Today, I invited Shame for a cup of coffee,
She arrived draped in shades of indigo—
A hue so deep, it echoed sorrow,
I asked her gently, "Why so blue?"

She sighed, her voice a trembling stream,
"Because I must be true,
A mirror to the things you hide,
A keeper of all you fear inside."

I gazed at her and softly spoke,
"It's not what you think, it's not the whole truth,
I am not the weight you make me bear,
It wasn't supposed to feel so unfair."

She looked at me with steady eyes,
"Yet here we are, bound in ties.
You cling to what you can't undo,
And I remain a part of you."

"But must you be so hard on me?" I asked,
"Don't I deserve a second chance?
What's done is done, the past is past,
Can't we rewrite this at last?"

Shame paused, her indigo dimmed,
And whispered, "Perhaps it's time to mend.
To live with integrity, you must see—
I am not your enemy, but your plea."

With that, we sat in quiet grace,
Two old foes, finding our place.
Over coffee, I learned this truth anew—
That growth begins when you befriend the blue.

29. The Seeker's Haven

In quiet halls where whispers dwell,
She finds her peace, her sacred spell.
A girl who walks with dreams untamed,
In books and words, her heart is named.

The pages turn, a gentle sound,
In every line, new worlds are found.
The more she reads, the more she sees,
A boundless sky, a boundless sea.

For in this quest, her love is returned,
In every tale, her spirit burned.
The library stands, her world, her throne,
A place where she is never alone.

Few pursuits can match this tender grace,
Where time dissolves, and thoughts embrace.
In books, she finds a love so true,
A haven where her soul renews.

The ink, it speaks, the paper sighs,
A symphony beneath the skies.
For every word, a piece of peace,
A quiet joy that will not cease.

Oh, seeker of the boundless lore,
Your heart will always crave for more.
In books, your love is never spurned,
A fire lit, a lesson learned.

So let the pages guide your way,
Through night and night, through day and day.
For in this world of ink and thought,
Your peace is found, and love is sought.

30. Maa, My World

Before the world, there was your womb,
A universe within that quiet room.
I knew the world through your embrace,
A heartbeat's rhythm, a sacred space.

As a child, I sought your arms,
A shelter safe from life's alarms.
The world outside, a storm, a fright,
But your love was my guiding light.

Irrational fears would grip me tight,
The unknown world, a daunting sight.
I'd shun it all, retreat, withdraw,
But you would push me, gently, raw.

"Go, my child, the world's not cruel,
You'll find your strength, you'll break the rule."
And though I'd stumble, though I'd fall,
I'd always return to you, my all.

For home was never walls or doors,
It was your love, my heart's soft core.
My world began and ended there,
In your embrace, beyond compare.

Every loss, every tear I cried,
Only drew me closer to your side.
Our bond grew stronger, deep and true,
A love unbroken, forever new.

If there's one thing in this world I'd claim,
One thing I'd cherish, one eternal flame,
It's you, Maa, my heart's own song,
The place where I've always belonged.

Maa, my world, my start, my end,
My dearest companion, my truest friend.
In your love, I find my way,
Forever and always, come what may.

31. The Fear

She walks unshaken through storms and fire,
Knows betrayal like an old, worn attire.
She does not flinch at sharpened lies,
Or the cold indifference in strangers' eyes.

But kindness—oh, that shakes her core,
A gentle touch she can't ignore.
Not the wounds, not the ones who deceive,
But those who stay, who never leave.

She knows the world, its ruthless game,
How quick they are to judge, to name.
Yet, here they stand, these rare, kind few,
Seeing her fully, seeing her true.

And that is what unsettles most—
Not the ghosts of pain, nor what she's lost,
But the way a hand, so soft, so light,
Could undo her walls in a single night.

She wonders—what is wrong with me?
Why does love feel like a tragedy?
Perhaps it's safer, standing alone,
Than risking a heart she's never known.

32. The Weight of Chance

"Do you ever question," she began, her gaze so deep,
"The privileges you hold, the promises you keep?"
He looked at her, confused, a flicker in his eye,
"Like what?" he asked, beneath the pale blue sky.

"The things we're given, without a choice or say,
Good parents' love, that brightens every day,
A decent upbringing, knowledge freely shared,
Opportunities that blossom, futures we've prepared.
Our faith, our name, the very ground we tread,
These gifts unearned, inside our hearts and heads."

He paused a while, considering her plea,
"I don't think about it quite as much as thee."
She sighed, a wisp of breath upon the breeze,
"Doesn't it touch you, this world's unease?
The children born to hardship, pain, and strife,
Dealt cruel hands, throughout their fragile life?"

"The universe is flawed," he said, with shrug and sigh,
"Indifferent, cold, beneath the endless sky.
Who are we mortals, to question cosmic fate?
This madness reigns, it's simply how things wait."

"I wish," she murmured, lost in distant thought,
"This world could be utopian, a haven dearly sought."
He smiled, a gentle curve upon his face,
"Leave that for books," he said, "a literary space."

33. Broken Mirror

A heart so open, brimming with gentle grace,
Saw in his eyes, a love she longed to embrace.
He seemed to mirror back the depths she felt,
A perfect match, a love that fate had dealt.

His charm, a mask, concealing what lay deep,
A hunger burning, promises to keep,
But only for the moment, for the
gain,
A master of illusion, playing love's sweet game.

Small cracks appeared, beneath the charming face,
A subtle coldness, in his warm embrace.
He'd twist her words, and turn them into lies,
A constant need for praise, behind disguise.

Her gentle spirit, he would manipulate,
A puppet on a string, sealed by cruel fate.
He'd drain her light, and feed upon her soul,
Leaving emptiness, taking its cruel toll.

She'd try to mend the pieces, understand,
The fractured love, slipping through her hand.
But every touch, a calculated sting,

A web of deceit, where shadows always cling.

A whisper of warning, deep inside her stirred,
But love, or what she thought it was, preferred
To blind her to the truth, the painful cost,
A fragile hope, already lost.

The storm erupted, tears began to fall,
Her open heart, breaking through it all.
He'd built her up, just to watch her descend,
A cruel satisfaction, until the bitter end.

Her love, so pure, so freely given, bright,
Misplaced, abused, extinguished by his light.
He never knew the depth of what he'd stole,
The selfless love, that made her spirit whole.

And in the ruins, where her dreams lay bare,
She learned a truth, in sorrow and despair.
That love like hers, so vulnerable and true,
Could not survive, the darkness he imbues.

34. Anxiety and Chaos

She was quiet, delicate, laced with fear,
A beautiful girl wrapped in brittle veneer.
Anxiety, they called her, a cautious delight,
A restless moon craving order at night.

He was wild, electric, a tempest untamed,
A handsome boy who laughed at the game.
Chaos, they called him, a fleeting spark,
A comet that burned through the endless dark.

She loved his fire, reckless and free,
The way he danced without guarantee.
He loved her stillness, fragile yet deep,
The way she felt everything, even in sleep.

But love is cruel when rhythm is lost—
When silence and storms are cruelly crossed.
She clung too tightly, fearing he'd leave,
He ran too fast, needing to breathe.

She planned, he strayed. She froze, he leapt.
She whispered reason, he barely slept.
She was the anchor, he was the tide—
Pulled together, yet worlds collide.

And so, it ended—not in a fight,
Not in fury, but fading light.
For love is fatal when it's misread—
When a restless heart meets a restless head.

35. The Girl Who Loved Rain

She was born to the sound of falling skies,
A child of thunder, of whispered sighs.
The rain was not just water to her,
But a song, a balm, a whispering cure.

When storms rolled in, she found her peace,
A quiet place where thoughts could cease.
She'd sit by the window for hours untold,
Watching silver threads weave stories old.

The pitter-patter, a lullaby sweet,
A rhythm her restless heart would meet.
It cleansed not just streets but something within,
Washing away where her worries had been.

For how often does the world seem new?
With trees so green, with skies so blue?
When dust is gone, when the earth is bright,
And the world, for a moment, feels just right.

So let it rain, let it pour,
Let it drench the earth once more.

For she was a girl who found her way,
In every storm, in every grey.

65

36. The Gorgeous Paradox

She walks the world, a quiet flame,
Soft in presence, fierce in name.
A mind that dreams, a heart that knows,
A spirit wild, yet calm, composed.

She longs for solitude, craves the deep,
Yet aches for souls she'll never keep.
A fortress built with walls so high,
Yet leaves the gate unlocked nearby.

She speaks in whispers, thinks in storms,
A rebel bound by duty's norms.
She yearns for truth, yet hides her own,
Most understood when left unknown.

She feels too much, yet stays so strong,
A wanderer who won't belong.
She leads with fire, yet shuns the light,
A guiding star lost in the night.

A dreamer's heart, a warrior's mind,
A seeker's soul, both fierce and kind.
She is the storm, she is the sea,
The gorgeous paradox—wild and free.

37. Love Should Breathe

Love was never meant to be chains,
Never a burden, never in vain.
Yet hands that clutch, that grasp too tight,
Turn warmth to suffocation, light into night.

Need is a shadow, heavy and wide,
A longing that swallows, a love misapplied.
It whispers, "Stay, don't leave my side,"
But love is lost where fear resides.

It does not lure hearts, nor make them stay,
It does not spark joy, but pulls it away.
For love is drawn to those who glow,
Not to those who beg it not to go.

To be needed is not to be adored,
It invites obligation, but never more.
For love should breathe, should rise, should roam—
Not feel like prison, but feel like home.

38. The Epidemic of Loneliness

Loneliness spreads like a silent disease,
Drifting through cities, carried by breeze.
Not seen, not heard, yet felt so deep,
A sickness that lingers, a wound that won't weep.

It starts as a whisper, soft in the mind,
A seat left empty, a moment unkind.
Then grows like ivy, twisting, tight,
Turning daylight into night.

And soon, it leaps from soul to soul,
An unseen fire, burning whole.
A glance avoided, a call ignored,
A world so crowded, yet hearts untethered, bored.

But oh, how kind, how rare, how bright,
When someone steps into your night.
A voice that breaks the looping chain,
A hand that pulls you from the rain.

"Come with me," they gently say,
"Join the world, just for today."
A nudge, a laugh, a moment shared,

And suddenly, the weight is spared.

For loneliness is an endless tide,
But love is the ship where hope can hide.
And only connection—warm and true,
Can heal the empty, and make us new.

39. The Craziest Thing

"What's the craziest thing you've done?" he teased,
"Apart from waiting for someone for a decade, at least?"
She laughed, a sound both light and sore,
"Nothing beats that—nothing more."

A pause, a glance, then came the ask,
"Do I look delusional, lost in the past?"
He met her eyes, steady and true,
"You look broken, but not confused."

"You're too wise to chase false dreams,
Too aware of what love means.
People do crazy things, it's true,
But why feel sorry for what love made you do?"

She smiled, half bitter, half relieved,
For in his words, she finally believed—
That loving too hard, for far too long,
Wasn't delusion. Just a love gone wrong.

40. Big Brother

He is the eldest, at least in name,
Yet wisdom's torch is mostly my claim.
I love him too much—can't stand him too,
The finest paradox I ever knew.

We don't need words, not every day,
But the moment we meet, we know what to say.
A glance, a sigh, the weight in his eyes—
I find out the truths he carefully hides.

And oh, the joy of making him squirm,
A generous bribe, a lesson well-learned.
"Keep this from Mom?" he pleads, resigned,
"What's in it for me?" I sweetly chime.

He calls himself the beauty divine,
Yet somehow that joke never feels mine.
My worst critic, sharp as a blade,
But my loudest cheer when doubts invade.

Sometimes I wonder, who's older here?
The roles we switch, so fluid, so clear.
Yet through it all, one thing is true –
In this chaotic world, he's my constant, my glue.

No matter the distance, the fights, the ride,
He is my family – my pride.

41. The Art of Breaking

"Have you ever had your heart broken?" he asked,
Casual, curious, as if love was the only task.

"Almost on a daily basis," she said with a sigh,
And he turned to her, puzzled, asking why.

"Daily?" he echoed, eyes open wide,
"Is it really that easy for heartaches to collide?"

She smiled, but it wasn't light or free,
It was laced with sorrow, as deep as the sea.

"My heart breaks when a song aches with pain,
When agony hums in every refrain.
When I read of a tragedy, fiction or not,
And feel for a world that time forgot."

"It shatters at injustice, the weight of the blind,
At war, at hunger, at mankind unkind.
When power crushes the ones with no name,
When suffering is normal, a rigged, cruel game."

"It breaks at the sight of a child with no home,
At a world that lets the forsaken roam.

At the apathy painted on every street,
At the kindness that dies beneath our feet."

"And people, of course, they break it too,
With words unspoken, with love untrue.
But maybe that's just what it means to be alive—
To break, to feel, to ache, to survive."

He watched her then, no words to say,
For what a rare thing, to break this way.

42. My Papa, My Silent Strength

In the quiet, I see you most,
not in grand words, not in boasts,
but in the steady way you stand,
a lighthouse carved by patient hands.

I see myself reflected in you,
in quiet thoughts and the things we do,
the way we feel more than we say,
the way we love without display.

When grief wrapped around my chest,
you did not rush, did not protest.
You stood beside me, calm and still,
holding space, bending will.

Not pushing joy, nor masking pain,
but reminding me again, again—
that happiness is not escape,
but a choice we gently shape.

When I grew tired, I found your shoulder,
a place of warmth as the world grew colder.
And softly, you whispered in my ear,

"Don't worry, I am here."

"We are all here, we always will be,"
your voice a shore, a quiet sea.
No love is greater, no truth more bright,
than a father's heart, steady and light.

Even on days I cannot see,
the girl you love inside of me,
you stand with pride, you stand so tall—
a father, a home, my safest wall.

43. Choosing Herself

She was the girl who always gave,
Who poured herself so others stayed.
A quiet light, a steady hand,
A shelter built on love unplanned.

She stitched their wounds, she bore their weight,
She held them up, she made them safe.
But somewhere lost in all she gave,
She forgot the life she, too, must save.

Self-love was foreign, self-care unknown,
A language she never called her own.
To choose herself felt cold, unkind,
A crime against the heart designed.

But now she walks a different way,
A path where she can heal, not fray.
It isn't easy, not at all,
Undoing years that made her small.

She stumbles, stops, then stands again,
Rewriting truths with shaking hands.
For loving herself is long overdue,
And this time—this time, she'll follow through.

44. The Home Within

I searched for home in distant lands,
In stranger's eyes, in reaching hands.
Through open doors and empty nights,
Through fleeting love and city lights.

I sat in cafés, lost in sound,
Hoping comfort could be found.
In laughter shared, in hands held tight,
In stories spun on quiet nights.

I chased the warmth in roads unknown,
Through noisy trains and flights, and crowds alone.
Yet every place, each face I knew,
Was just a mirror, shining through.

For all I sought, so far, so wide,
Was always waiting—deep inside.

45. The Four Who Will Find You

"You will meet them all, my dear," she said,
"There's no path where they won't tread.
Fated threads, unseen yet tight,
They'll come to you when the time is right."

Soul Mates will find you first,
A love so deep, a soothing verse.
A friend, a partner, a bond so true,
A piece of home in someone new.

Kindred Spirits cross your way,
Echoes of you in things they say.
They share your fire, your dreams, your fight,
A guiding star on the darkest night.

Then comes the flame, the Twin so rare,
A soul split once, now laid bare.
A mirror sharp, intense and bright,
They break, they build, they bring new light.

And when you least expect, Karmic ties appear,
Some bring joy, some bring tears.
Lessons wrapped in love or pain,

To free your soul, to break your chain.

"You cannot hide, you cannot flee,
They are written into your destiny.
So meet them well, embrace, let go,
Each one will shape the you you'll know."

46. The Quizmaster's Lesson

She sat in silence, heart worn thin,
A weight too heavy, a war within.
Loneliness curled in the space besides,
A quiet ache she couldn't hide.

He saw the sorrow, felt the weight,
And knew that words would come too late.
So instead, he built a game,
A quiz of stories, loss, and fame.

Movies first—she barely spoke,
Lost in thought as the questions broke.
Then came books—her eyes grew bright,
A flicker of fire, a spark of light.

She answered one, then two, then three,
And for a moment, she felt free.
Among strangers, yet not alone,
For words had made this place her own.

And when the game had reached its close,
He smiled and spoke, the lesson rose—
"Life moves forward, never back,"
"No rewind, no faded track."

"It may be tough, the road may bend,
But trust me, this is not the end."

She looked at him, a tear, a sigh,
And in that moment, she knew he'd tried.
Not with empty words or grand display,
But with a quiz that lit her way.

47. What Remains

I had read once—how life grows around grief,
How time does not erase, only reshapes the ache.
And then, I felt it myself.

Grief stepped in where love once stood,
Filling the space with silence, with void.
It whispered absence in rooms too full of memories,
In laughter that no longer reached my eyes.

The mind is cruel in its remembering—
Summoning the good, the bad, the unbearable,
At moments when I am least prepared
To hold the weight of what was lost.

But in time, I stopped resisting the emptiness.
I let it sit beside me, a quiet companion,
Neither friend nor foe, but something known.
And somehow, I made peace with the void.

They say life is an endless act of letting go—
And one day, even life itself will end.
But what remains is not the leaving,
Not the absence, not the wounds,
But the love I once held, the stories I keep,

The echoes of those who shaped me.

I do not try to fight it, I do not try to forget.
Instead, I have learned to carry my grief well,
Not as a burden, but as proof—
That I have loved, that I have lost,
And that I have survived.

48. Ek Cutting Chai

A morning cup, warm and bright,
Steaming hope in golden light.
With Maa besides, the world feels new,
Tea and love, a bond they brew.

10 AM, the desk awaits,
A sip, a pause, a list of fates.
To-do's unfold in caffeine's grace,
Work and tea, a steady pace.

4 PM, a soft rewind,
A moment to leave the rush behind.
A day well spent, a breath, a smile,
Tea in hand, rest awhile.

6:30 strikes, the laughter flows,
Colleagues turned friends; the chatter grows.
Stories spill with every pour,
Chai, the bridge that bonds us more.

In stress, it soothes; in joy, it sings,
A silent friend in suffering.
A binding wine, a sacred space,
Where anguish, dreams, and plans embrace.

From habit to ritual, thread by thread,
Tea became the life she led.
Seamless, effortless, forever nigh,
Her soul steeped deep in ek cutting chai.

49. Forgiveness Begins at Home

Forgiveness, like charity, starts within,
A quiet act to mend the fractures within skin.
It's not for the world, nor for those who stray,
But for the self-that's lost along the way.

The parts you hide, the choices you rue,
The years you think were wasted, untrue—
They linger like shadows, heavy and dim,
Yet forgiveness whispers, "Make peace with him."

The you who stumbled, the you who fell,
The you who walked through your own hell—
They are not flaws, but threads in the weave,
A tapestry only you can believe.

Contradictions dance, a chaotic art,
The messy, the broken, the tender heart.
To love what's unlovable, to hold it tight,
Is to rescue yourself in the darkest night.

Forgiveness is not for others to give,
It's the act of learning how to live
With the weight of the past, the scars, the pain,

And finding the strength to breathe again.

So be gentle, dear soul, with the you that you see,
The one in the mirror, longing to be free.
Forgive the missteps, the doubts, the strife—
For forgiveness is the compass to your own life.

It's not betrayal to love what's flawed,
To embrace the cracks where the light is clawed.
It's a rescue, a temporary calm, a tender start—
Forgiveness begins in the chambers of your heart.

50. Moving On – My Heart's Journey

They say moving on is a straight path,
a clean break, a single night's math.
But it's not a door you simply shut—
it's a mosaic of what was and what's cut.

It's gathering shards of a heart once whole,
pieces scattered, each with its own role.
The sharp edges of love, the jagged lines of pain,
the fragments of joy you'd do it all for again.

You glue them together, but it's never the same.
The cracks remain, each one with a name.
A reminder of laughter, of tears, of the fight,
of the way you loved with all your might.

It's not the heart you started with, no—
it's been reshaped by the highs and the low.
It's softer in places, harder in others,
a patchwork of lessons, of lovers, of mothers.

You hold it up to the light and see,
the beauty in its broken symmetry.
It's not perfect, but it's still yours,

a testament to love's open doors.

Yes, it aches, and yes, it still hurts,
but it's also a map of where you've been, of your worth.
The good, the bad, the ugly, the true—
they all live in this heart, renewed.

So when he asks how it feels to move on,
you say it's not about the hurt being gone.
It's about holding the pieces, both dark and bright,
and knowing you're stronger for the love and the fight.

It's about seeing the cracks and still feeling whole,
about honouring the journey, the scars, the soul.
Because even in the ache, there's a beauty that stays—
a heart that loved, and will love again, someday.

51. The Girl Who Wrote Her Heartache

She sat with sorrow, heavy and deep,
A heart in fragments, wounds that wouldn't sleep.
Love had left her, a shadow of its past,
A fleeting dream that faded too fast.

But in her hands, she held a pen,
A quiet weapon to fight the pain within.
She wrote of nights that stretched too long,
Of broken chords in a once-loved song.

Each word a tear, each line a sigh,
She poured her grief beneath the sky.
The page became her confidant,
A place where hurt could freely rant.

Months went by, her notebook filled,
With verses born from wounds she'd spilled.
Her heartache turned to ink and rhyme,
A tapestry woven through space and time.

One day she sat, her voice unsure,
In a room where healing sought a cure.
Her psychiatrist listened, his gaze so kind,

As she shared the poems she'd left behind.

He smiled softly, leaned in to say,
"What you've done is a rare display.
Sublimation—a gift, a defence,
Turning pain to art, it's profound, immense."

"When sorrow strikes, and the world feels bleak,
You channel it into words, unique.
Not all can transform their grief this way,
But you've found beauty in the disarray."

Her eyes lit up, a spark anew,
A truth uncovered, a perspective true.
Her heartache wasn't just a weight to bear,
But a muse that crafted something rare.

Now she writes with purpose, with light,
Her pain no longer a endless night.
For in her hands, the pen still gleams,
A tool to heal, to mend her dreams.

And so she thrives, her spirit free,
A poet of grief, of artistry.
For in the depths of her broken start,
She found the alchemy of the heart.

www.ingramcontent.com/pod-product-compliance
Lightning Source LLC
LaVergne TN
LVHW011036200726

843509LV00011B/1290